T0374400

DOWN
SOUTH & OTHER PLACES

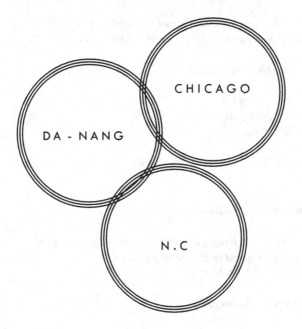

DA - NANG

CHICAGO

N.C

ERIC KOPLIN

authorHOUSE®

AuthorHouse™
1663 Liberty Drive
Bloomington, IN 47403
www.authorhouse.com
Phone: 1 (800) 839-8640

© 2018 Eric Koplin. All rights reserved.

No part of this book may be reproduced, stored in a retrieval system, or transmitted by any means without the written permission of the author.

Published by AuthorHouse 02/24/2018

ISBN: 978-1-5462-2946-9 (sc)
ISBN: 978-1-5462-2944-5 (hc)
ISBN: 978-1-5462-2945-2 (e)

Library of Congress Control Number: 2018902050

Print information available on the last page.

Any people depicted in stock imagery provided by Getty Images are models, and such images are being used for illustrative purposes only. Certain stock imagery © Getty Images.

This book is printed on acid-free paper.

Because of the dynamic nature of the Internet, any web addresses or links contained in this book may have changed since publication and may no longer be valid. The views expressed in this work are solely those of the author and do not necessarily reflect the views of the publisher, and the publisher hereby disclaims any responsibility for them.

SUMMARY

Down South and Other Places is a non-fiction work by (Eric Koplin).
He tells a tale of being a support troop (heavy equipment operator) in
Vietnam in 1969. He was an enlisted man, a Lance Corporal (E3) in
the United States Marine Corps. He moves around southern I Corps
providing support to infantry units. His stories are about the craziness
of that era and place. He then takes us home to Chicago, Illinois and the
western suburbs of that great city. He tells us stories of how a 19-year-old
veteran was treated in 1970. He tells us a bit of how he adjusted and he
touches on his Post Traumatic Stress Disorder (PTSD) and depression
which he deals with to this day.

He tells of friends, people in general, and Veterans Hospitals and staff.
The book sums up the uselessness of that war and the awful treatment
our returning veterans endured at the hands of their fellow Americans.

ACKNOWLEDGEMENTS

I need to thank so many people. First of all my wife of 43 years whose support I could not have done this without. My three children who never gave up on Dad, even when Dad was crazy, down and out. My veteran service officers, social workers and psychiatrists who all knew me better than I know myself. I fought against their diagnoses for years; only to find out they were right, I did have depression and PTSD and still do. My brother who encouraged me to write, many friends in vet centers, V.A. hospitals and last but not least my local DAV. Please forgive me for not naming names, there are just too many. Your names are in my heart, if not here on paper. All of you know who you are and you all contributed to my growth and well-being. People who edited and proof read, typed and helped me so much. My main doctor at Salisbury, NC VA hospital. Thank you Doc! And my higher power who I call Jesus Christ. Thank you Jesus.

PROLOGUE

This work, as short as it is, was written over a period of many years. I first started writing in PTSD treatment because I couldn't speak well in group. So I wrote things down. Then my doctor asked to read my notes to the whole wing in the dayroom once a day. They liked it. This gave me a big head and I thought maybe I could write a book. Well, I'm no English major and I don't spell too well, but I found people who would help me with that. Like I already said, the vets liked my stories, but then that was a concern too. Would anyone other than vets like my notes? I had to find out so here it is for you, hope you like it. I was on the PTSD wing of Salisbury, NC VA hospital being treated. I have PTSD and major depression. But this is not a PTSD book or a Vietnam book per se. It's a life story of war, peace and addiction. It's a work of non-fiction. I'm proud to be a Marine and Vietnam Vet. I'm proud to be an American. I believe we have the best country going. Well, don't take yourselves too seriously and please enjoy!

PART I

PART 1

1969

OKI WAS A strange place for a newly turned 18 year old. Oki was transit-five days tops and then down South. What a remarkable culture. These little Oriental people seemed to be thousands of years behind us. I stayed on base mostly; had to make a couple of formations a day to see if I had a flight number down South yet. The base was like no base I'd ever seen. The club had slot machines and mixed drinks. I drank a lot of something I'd never heard of before; Singapore Slings. Pretty Okinawan waitresses brought them to you while live bands played on stage. I got so drunk one night, I couldn't find my barracks so I passed out in front of the club. Our barracks was a "no frills" open squad bay. All I had was transistor radio. Us new guys were easy to spot and everybody asked, "Going down South, going down South?" "Yeah, I don't know when, soon." "You know Da-Nang Airstrip is destroyed? You know MOS doesn't matter, you'll have to fight as soon as you deplane." Rumors, nothing but rumors. Have a little fun with the new guys. The vets in Oki that were coming from down South were different. They looked old and very tan, but it was the eyes. Their eyes looked through you. I couldn't help but wonder if I lived, if I would look like that. One day I was lying in the rack, my transistor on Armed Forces Radio. Donovan was singing about Atlantis. These two vets came over and asked me if they could just stand there and listen. "Yeah, sure," I said. They did, and when the song was over they left without a word. Viet-nam vets were strange; strange I tell you. Two days later we flew into Da-Nang. Two F4 Phantom jets escorted our airliner in. No, the runways were not torn up and we didn't fight our way in. But yes, I was scared, very scared.

I JUST GOT HERE

SGT. BEAR WAS on his knees praying Hell, I don't know. I just got here. Is he praying? He's got to be, shall we say, concerned. L/Cpl. pissed off? L/Cpl. in charge! L/Cpl. Wildman? Hell, I don't know his name, remember, I just got here! Real life drama, man! Tension-thick, almost as bad as the humidity here. Is someone laughing? Is that sky on the perimeter purple? Can't be, it's 12 o'clock at night. That's not purple, THAT'S RED, DEEP BLOOD RED and it stinks! No, uh-uh, no, I won't accept that. What's out there? Is that a battle going on or lights or what? FUCK! I can't comprehend this shit, yet, ever, please Lord never. My rifle wouldn't work. Sgt. Andover took it, brought it back, was pissed at me, said it wouldn't work. I just got it this afternoon, you gotta remember. I just got here. The dispatcher in the Jeep, with Sgt. Andover, said L/Cpl. Wildman let Bear live. I got to sleep in the shop bunker tonight. I can't go out to the perimeter yet because yes, that's right, I just got here!

EXPENDABLE PEOPLE, EXPENDABLE GEAR

THAT DOZER BACK in from Go Noi Island? Yep, that's it. (Go Noi Island, adjacent to Dodge City, a hot spot known well to the Marines of Southern I [Eye] Corps.). 1st Shore Party Bn. had a few pieces of heavy equipment on an operation there in the summer of '69. (The grunts sweep the area, the combat engineers look for booby traps and unexploded ordinance and then the heavy equipment goes in to clear land and dig up and fill in enemy bunkers). "Yeah, well," Sgt. says, "Get somebody to steam clean it off." Well, nobody would. The dozer was still mechanically sound, just dirty and messy. Messy with L/Cpl. Darrington. Darrington was backing his dozer through a tree line and an NVA soldier with an RPG hit him square in the chest with a rocket grenade. Didn't hurt the dozer much. So, the dozer sat covered with little bits of a Marine operator. Finally, somebody steam cleaned it. Some new guy who didn't know nothing, probably. The dozer sat in the back of the lot and nobody

would run it. Bad vibes, jinxed. As far as the operators were concerned,

it was as dead as Darrington. Don't know what ever happened to that

dozer. Rumor has it that it was buried, written off as a combat loss. Does

the U.S. Military waste tax dollars? Sure they do, but not this time, I

don't think. Seems to me quite the right thing. It was Darrington's dozer

period. He's not around to run it, then nobody else should either. Costly?

Sure! But how much does one lousy old dozer cost compared to bombs

being dropped, etc; and people like Darrington. What do they cost?

They cost their families and friends. They cost this nation. Men like that

would have benefitted the country once they were back home. What does

a young man cost? Fuck the dozer. Bury it and forget it. Bury the young

men, but don't ever forget them and their sacrifices.

THE REAR

LIKE SGT. PEPPER'S Lonely Hearts Band, some time off, not too hot today, cammie trousers, no shirt, Ho Chi Men sandals, fans in the hootch (tent), beer, my bros singing, "Everybody's Smoking Pot," laid back feeling, talk of home, talk of girls and cars, fast cars, faster women, food, yeah man, pizza or a cheeseburger. Henry, slow-talking, good-hearted Henry, just back in from Dodge. "Is that a hair on your chest? Hey guys, a hair!" He reaches out and pulls. My one and only chest hair. "You're growing up" Henry says. "Ah, yeah," I say, mourning my loss of hair. "What a place to do it" he says. Somewhere deep inside, red lights flashed, warning bells sounded reality. Oh shit, that's right, he's right. Well, let's just put that thought somewhere else, certainly wouldn't want to think about that today. The Beatles were singing about a yellow submarine. Allen was talking about his girlfriend in that Rhode Island accent of his. Pauly, wild-eyed, dirty-looking Pauly was looking under the floor for roaches and I was not going to think about growing up. But a chord had been struck. I believe that's the day I became more insecure and sometimes stuttered a little, sometimes. Who was the walrus anyway?

ANOTHER RUN

CHARLIE TOOK OUT a cow today. I was back in character, my element, if you please. Red dusty road, vacuum sound of a Detroit diesel with a 4-71 running a little hot. 7.82 gear swinging from the headache bar, M-16 tucked behind the seat, six frags in the toolbox, foot to the floor. Don't want to hit a mine going slow. I can see the hill up ahead. In the distance, choppers swarming in and out like bees around a hive, red dust swirling up to the clouds. Landing zone Payne, Hill 55, home of 7th Marines. Behind it, the Arizona, Charlie Ridge Marine Corps Lore, well, I'm starting to ramble on here, got to slow down, got a left turn to make. Lot of the little people outside the gate, some kind of commotion going on. Slow down, down to a crawl, right side of the road blocked with people. A.R.V.N. running around shooting in the air, farmers shouting, waving their arms. What's wrong with this picture? I'm searching, looking for danger, taking everything in, all my senses turned all the way up. Creeping slowly by, I see her scared eyes, labored breathing, her whole side full of holes. Probably a box mine. I probably should have shot her, someone maybe did, I don't know. I kept going. Later sometime, I can't remember when, I realized there had been no traffic. Only me and the cow, so now I regret not ending her suffering. I mean, hell, she took the mine I probably would've hit. Thank you Bossey, hope there is a reward for cows someplace. Charlie-1, Cow-0. Payback's a motherfucker!

THE NEW X.O.

1st S.P. Bn. Rear area

Got a shower unit

Got a chow hall

Got a club

Got plenty of beer

Got nice hootches with tape decks and fans

Got a fairly large perimeter

Got eleven posts, some towers, some bunkers

Got a pretty secure area here

Got rockets and snipers, that's all

6 p.m. until 6 a.m. all Vietnamese people have to stay home, anything moving outside the wire during those hours is apt to get shot. Well, good old 1st S.P. Bn. Rear had an exception to that rule. There was a mama-san with about five girls who would roam up and down the perimeter around 6 p.m. Yelling through the wire at each post, "Who wants 'boom boom'?" Now folks, when a Viet.woman asks if you want "boom boom," she means, "Do you want sex?" No, sorry fellows, it's cheap, but it ain't free. There was a couple of ways to do it. If a post said they wanted two girls, then two girls would hide in the bushes near that post and the Marines would either slip into the bushes after dark, or they would slip the girls into the post. Posts were checked at night by the O.D., so leaving the girls in the bushes was the safest. The girls would stay in the bushes all night go home after 6 a.m. when people could move about again. These girls were not your Saigon-type hookers. These were peasant girls from nearby villages. They had no fancy clothes or make-up. They had regular pajama-type outfits and most of them chewed beetlenut. Some even had gook sores and venereal diseases were pretty common among them. I never indulged in this activity myself, but I saw the girls and heard the stories and it was rather sad. The

chaplain used to say the venereal disease rate in the battalion was much higher in number than his congregation on Sundays. One afternoon, I arrived on post about 5:30 p.m. and the new X.O. was inspecting the condition of the area, checking things out. He was awful young-looking for a Marine Major. He hopped out of his Jeep between posts and there was mama-san and four of her girls on their rounds. She was checking things out and inspecting the area also. Well, our new X.O. called to her and went outside the wire to talk to her, we couldn't hear the conversation, but it was definitely heated discussion. Suddenly, the new X.O. had mama-san by the arm and was slapping the shit out of her. He hit her pretty good. I didn't enjoy watching an old woman get slapped silly. The new X.O. strutted back to his Jeep warning mama-san no to come around with her girls anymore. We settled in, checked our radio, last minute weapons check, chose watches and settled down to shoot the bull. Conversation was centered around the whooping mama-san got. Mostly, everyone agreed that the new X.O. was a real jerk. By about 2 a.m. I doubt there was a post on the perimeter that hadn't received sniper fire. Mana-san probably had a V.C. papa-san or baby-san or maybe mama-san herself wielded a mean AK-47. Ducking rounds on post wasn't fun, luckily none of us were hit that night. I don't

believe I ever saw the new X.O. around the perimeter again and mama-

san and her girls were back on the job in about three days. We were

definitely winning the hearts and minds of the people. Yessiree Bob,

we were winning this war. Hey, maybe we'll all be home for Christmas!

ONE NIGHT

WAS ASLEEP, YOU understand. Middleton burst in yelling, throwing things. Michael followed. "Was it the new guys? Was it the new guys?" "It doesn't matter Michael, it doesn't fucking matter. New, old, in-between, it don't fucking matter! They killed him, they fucking killed him!" I was awake now, not fully. I didn't want to be awake fully. I didn't want to even be in here with this. This is bad! Don't know what yet, but this is bad! Middleton was shaking and burning leeches off his legs, more than shaking really, he was jumping around having chills, complaining about leeches. "Are there any on my back? Are there any on my back? Oooohh, leeches. I hate leeches!" Post #6 had been assaulted. They came across a field of rice paddies at around 3 a.m. running, charging, yelling at the top of their lungs. At least I think they were yelling. I believe Middleton said he was yelling, but I'm not sure. I was sound asleep. Post #6, secure post. Post #6, right across from Dog Patch, never been assaulted before?! But the Marines on Post #6 were ready, ready Freddie! Nobody gonna take Post #6. Moonless night, "dark, baby, dark." Post #6 let's go a "pop-up." "Pop" daylight, eerie flare daylight. Who was the kid on the sixty? Nobody knows, but he didn't waste no time "getting some." Spent shells flying around Post #6, M-60 chattering its deadly machine gun music, M-16's pop, pop, popping. The assaulting squad, caught! Caught big time. Open field, all lit up, M-16's and a sixty spitting lead at them. One man killed instantly, face down in the muddy leech-filled paddy water. Yeah bro, leeches. Fucking no good, blood-sucking, slimy leeches. Middleton got his leeches off now. He's crying and I've got to get back to sleep. I'm tired. Tired from work, tired of this shit, tired man. You know, tired! I was walking between the hootches today on my way to chow and I heard some shitbird say to another, "I think I'll write that kid's mom and tell her the truth man, she oughta know." I didn't say nothing, just kept heading for chow. Hope he didn't though. Hope he didn't.

ROCK BIG ROCK

I T'S FUNNY ABOUT heroes. Big Rock was a hero, 'course he don't think so. But there's a few who know. On a dark night when nothing went right, Rock went to the side of a fallen brother. His brother was pale and Rock didn't recognize him, matter of fact, his brother was a stranger. Rock picked him up with those oak-like arms. Determination sat on his ebony face. With mud sucking at his feet, Rock started a dangerous journey home. Rock carried his bro in, past Post #6 without getting so much as a scratch. We all know now what happened that moonless night at Post #6. Nobody told Rock thanks, no medal hung on Rock's barrel chest. I don't think it was even mentioned again. But there's a few that know, and God knows, Rock. God knows. It's sometimes funny about heroes.

DOZER SECTION
H.E. PLT.

DAVE HIT AN explosive today. He was operating wearing his flak jacket and helmet. None of the others did, too hot. We don't know what he hit, 250 lb bomb maybe, anti-tank mine. Don't know? It tossed the Dozer about a foot in the air, blew off the right track and rollers, cracked the blade in half. I wasn't there, all I know is he lived. Shrapnel scraped across his forehead and dented his helmet. His whole face was bloody. The corpsman was afraid to take his helmet off. Afraid of what he might see, and I'll be, all Dave had was a scraped forehead and one hell of a headache. He gave the peace sign to the guys as the med evac chopper flew him out. Three days later he was back in the rear with us. He got a Purple Heart and a scar. Cool, huh? Yeah right. Another day, another little story. Go Noi Island, 1969.

THE NIGHT THE
MONEY CHANGED

MONEY MAKES THE world go round. So, I shouldn't have been surprised, but I was naïve, still full of duty ad honor and thought we had a cause. Little things kept happening that would chip away those feelings, but the night the money changed was a real eye opener. Troops all over Viet-nam used M.P.C. Funny money, monopoly money, play money, all little bills, no coins. You had 5¢ bills and 10¢ bills and 25¢ bills. You could have a wad of bills and still not have a lot of money. Now, I wasn't so naïve that I didn't realize that some people make money off of wars and that Viet-nam had drug dealers and prostitutes. All societies have their dregs. Well, anyways, the U.S. Military realized the Vietnamese had gotten their hands on a lot of M.P.C. and this was a no-no. So, without warning, they changed the money. Now, us troops could turn in our old M.P.C. and be issued new M.P.C., but Viet civilians couldn't, because they weren't supposed to have any in the first place. So, a lot of Vietnamese people went from riches to rags overnight. Now I realize that's a bummer, but I was taught a few things about ill-gotten gains, which I still believe Anyways, I was on guard duty that night, and oh man, the whole 1st Marine Division Area lit up. We got rockets and snipers like crazy. Every Vietnamese in the Da-Nang area must have picked up an AK-47 that night. I mean, wow, I thought we were here to help these folks, and they're so fickle, they're hitting us because of money change. Oh well, just like they say, our motto here. The unappreciated, doing the impossible for the uncaring.

WEED SEED THREATENS

SITTING OUT ON Post #8. Never liked Post #8. There was a Vietnamese cemetery right in front of it, and it wouldn't surprise me one bit if we weren't sitting on a few graves ourselves. It was a foggy night and some sort of Viet. Holiday. They were shooting off fireworks and it made us all a little jumpy. I propped my M-16 up on the bunker's wooden ledge along with extra mags within reach. Anything came through that fog, I wanted to be ready. The other guys all did the same, except one, I can't remember his name to save my life, but he was a rich kid. He was always bragging about how much he had at home. Well, he said "If anybody comes through that fog, I'm out of here!" which caused us all to say, "What?!" It's a smart move sometimes to get out of a bunker that the enemy know is there and fighting from one of the nearby fighting holes, but that's not what old rich boy meant, he meant he was gonna break and run. Now, I've never seen anybody run off before, but we would need all the fire power we had. So, to me it was a fire power issue. Well, Weed Seed was the senior man that night, and he told old rich kid right off the bat, "Look man, if you go for that bunker door I'll wax your ass off myself." I'm 100% sure old Weed Seed would have done it too. Well, it was quite a foggy night and nothing happened. But I thought it was funny that the rich kid wore a machete in his belt for about a week after that because he was afraid of Weed Seed. The rear was a real trip, yes, a real trip. Guys were always threatening each other. You'd go to sleep to the sound of drunks looking and loading on each other and racial tension was high. The rear really sucked. I spent as little time there as possible. I'd rather get blown away by Charlie than some drunk or high Marine. Everyone on the fire-bases were pretty tight. The rear was as tight as a bag of soup. I guess it was okay if you had some rank, but I didn't, so the Landing Zones were more like the real Corps. Semper Fi Mac.

MY LICENSE

I WENT TO CAMP Lejeune, NC for heavy equipment school. It was on a section of base called Courthouse Bay. We operated bulldozers and scrappers mainly. There was some equipment we only got familiarized on, a day on road graders, forklifts and cranes. They concentrated on three types of bulldozers, TD 15's, TD 18's and EMCO 130's. Scrappers were the nine yard pull type. Civilians had motorized scrappers, not so for the Corps. It was a three month school. We had plenty of written classes and on the job preventative maintenance and operating. We would operate all morning, wash and do preventative maintenance in the afternoons. Weekends were off. I graduated 6 out of 30. I was licensed for three bulldozers with attachments. After school I headed to Okinawa and Viet-nam. At Da-Nang I was assigned to the 1st Shore Party Bn. 1st Marine Division. A PFC (E-2), I had only been in seven months. 1st S.P. Bn. supported helicopters with H.S.T. teams. They had three letter company's; ALPHA, BRAVO and CHARLIE were H.S.T.

Then they had H&S Company making four company's (one battalion)

Headquarters and Service Company, that was us. A small platoon of

clerks and cooks, a small platoon of motor transport and a small engineer

attachment. I checked in and supply warehouse was on the ground. The

ammo dump (ASP one) had blown up a couple weeks earlier knocking

down some of our buildings. 1st S.P. Bn. was located three miles from Da-

Nang airstrip at a place called Freedom Hill (hill 327). Freedom Hill has

the best PX complex in I (eye) corps. The problem was it was destroyed

when the dump blew. It would take months to rebuild. Down the road

(Hwy 1) was 1st Medical Bn., 1st Recon Bn and then headquarters. 1st

Marine Division area had a PX, so anyway I checked into H&S Co. and

was assigned to H.E. Plt. as a 1345 heavy equipment operator. I reported

to an old salty-top (Master Sgt.). He asked as to what I was licensed for.

I told him bulldozers. He said "Good. You're in forklift section." I had

only operated an RTF 6000 (rough terrain forklift) for half a day in

school. I told Top I was not qualified on that piece of gear. He said there

were some old pallets on the back lot and to grab a lift and start learning.

For a week I did nothing but pick up pallets with the 6000. I was told forklifts section was safer than dozer section, 'cause dozers cleared bush.

Okay cool, but I didn't know anything yet. I didn't even know where our own perimeter was yet. They would not let a FNG go out there. I also ran a steam jenny, cleaning H.E. gear. It was 100° in Da-Nang and I was eating salt tabs like crazy and getting quite the tan. I was not sleeping well because it was so hot and I was scared at night, some night rockets would land around our area. We would have to run for bunkers. After a month of rear area training I was ready to go to the field. Top said he was sending me to Hill 55 south of Da-Nang to run lifts on the landing zone. The lifts were already there; all I had to do was catch a bird or convoy out to the hill. I didn't know what to think, but that didn't matter, I was going. I hopped on a convoy to the hill. I was wide-eyed at the Viet countryside and villages. I arrived and found the LZ. There was a hootch right next to a large LZ. LZ Payne 1st Shore Party Bn. Charlie Co. the sign read. A small sign above the hootch door said, H.E. PLT., "If we can't lift it, fuck it!" It was dusty and choppers were coming and going in front of me. Marlow was in charge of cranes and Mike in charge of lifts. L/Cpl. Florida was a crane operator and me and Sgt. Mike were the lift operators. That's it. Two sergeants, two troops and Doc our corpsman.

He was attached to the LZ also. He didn't stay long, he was replaced after an incident where a Marine grunt was killed on the LZ and Doc wasn't around. The grunts swore revenge against Doc and they flew him out. Bummer, shit happened, don't mean nothing. That was what everyone said, "don't mean nothing," yes it did mean something; but you would lose your mind if you thought about everything going on. Fire fights near the hill, green and red tracer rounds at night. Choppers going in and out amongst rounds. F-4 Phantoms and other aircraft pulling airstrikes over the hill, us receiving rockets and being on alert some nights. I sound like a POG compared to a grunt, (I was a POG [people other than grunts]) and it got to you a little, and you thanked your lucky stars you weren't a grunt. I had great respect for our infantry and took pride in supporting them. Well, the front gate of Hill 55 had a Gook laundry, you could drop your clothes off and they washed them in rice paddy water and fold them, wrap them in plastic. You could pick them up in a couple of days. We all had (sometimes), cans of Right Guard deodorant. After you got your clothes back you laid them out and sprayed them down. They still stank but not as bad. We did have a shower also. An aircraft belly tank was filled with water and sat atop a homemade stall. A welder installed a tap and you could turn the tap and gravity did its job. Aw, the rear! Well, I used my lift as my P.O.V. and I drove to the laundry. It was very uneven ground around the road by the laundry shack, so I parked on an angle and turned in my seat and I'll be damned the lift started falling over. I jumped as far from the lift as I could. I was facing away from it as it fell and the earth shook and a dust cloud covered me. I looked around and the headache bar was about two feet from my back. The Gooks started yacking and running around. I crawled under it and shut it off. A six by truck wrapped a chain to the headache bar and pull me right side up. It bent the headache bar a little, otherwise everything was fine. I drove back to the LZ and told them what happened. They told me to take the headache bar off and lay it by the LZ and we will say a truck hit it. Well, Top came out for a visit and Sgt. Marlow told him I turned a lift over. Top went back to Da-Nang and sent for me. I got back to Top's office and he said "Give me your forklift license." I informed I didn't have one. He called his dispatcher and said to him to type me up a 6000 license. Then he gave it to me and said "Here, next time you turn over a lift I'll tear that up. Now get back to that hill." So I got my 6000 license, went to the club and had a few cold ones before returning to Hill 55.

DYSENTERY

AD IT TWICE in Viet-nam. Once on Hill 55 when I was a FNG. Went through my cammies and had to wear tiger shorts. I lost weight, which at 130 lbs, I really didn't have any to lose. Was so sick and weak but had to operate anyway. Trunks of ammo came in every morning. We would get a convoy of at least 14 trucks a day, full of projectiles we called PRO-JO's. They were for the eight inch and 105 guns. Also, were flares, hand grenades and rifle rounds. All has to be unloaded and put in the ammo berms. Those fire bases like 55 used quite a bit of ammo. A couple of hours unloading and then break time until the choppers started coming loading and unloading their supplies. Cargo nets has to be loaded and unloaded drums of gasoline, diesel, C-rats, boots, cammies and etc. I lived in the head during those two weeks of dysentery. I got it from washing in the river I believe, but it could have been the food. My Sgt. Would let me sleep late when I needed to be up doing PM's on the lifts, needed to keep them rolling. Sgt. Marlow didn't like my sleeping in and he told me so, thought I was just goofing off. The Doc gave me something but dysentery has to run its course. Well, Hill 55 was home to the 7th Marine Regiment. They worked off the hill. 1st Tank Bn., a motor T and various supports units like FLC (Force Logistics Command) had a unit there. We stole a lot of our C-rats from FLC. We would make C-rat stew using nearly a whole case. Delicious, a couple beers a day, C-rats, cot, hootch and we lived pretty good. We overloaded a cargo net of gas and diesel fuel one afternoon and the chopper cut it loose. If a net is loaded wrong it could bring down a chopper. It fell in a rice paddy next to the hill. We could not operate in paddies or carry the 55 gallon drums back up; the radio operator on the LZ happened to get ahold of an OV-10 Bronco aircraft who was on his way back to Da-Nang airstrip and had a few rockets and 20mm ammo left onboard. He said he would swing by and destroy if for us. We gathered on the perimeter for the show. Marine Corps aviators are good, but sometimes, well, he missed the net with his rockets, came around and fired the cannon and still did not hit that net. So we called a tank (M-48) up from 1st tanks and the turret and angle was wrong for shooting downhill so the tank machine gunner was able to hit it and set that net on fire. Charlie wasn't gonna have that fuel! But I bet we spent a million dollars destroying that net. Oh well, war is costly right? That was an entertaining day on the hill and we drew our two beers and discussed our adventure. That night intel reports said a sapper platoon. was operating in our area so we had to stay awake; we got a few rockets that night that did little damage. I liked 55, I could have done my whole tour there. But on to other places.

TOP'S GOT IT

I WAS ASSIGNED A job out near Marble Mountain. Amtracs were moving out, changing areas, going home, I can't remember which, but they were in a hurry. They were sharing an area with 2/1. It was a fairly secure place near the base of the mountain. I arrived and immediately went to work. Their whole supply had to be loaded on trucks. They had a huge warehouse and a storage lot full of Amtrac parts. Flatbed trailers were dropped off empty for me every day and I'd load them up as quick as I could and they would be exchanged for more empties. Seemed like the cycle had no end there for a while. I was loading day and night. The large Rough Terrain Lifts (most all military heavy junk), have small lights called blackout lights. You're supposed to use them at night so you don't stand out so much. Sorry folks, they just don't get it when you are trying to load gear on trucks. I'd have to turn on my floodlights, get a quick peep of the pallet and forks and shut them off, drive to the trailer, hit the lights for a peep and kill them again. Not a real comfortable feeling doing that, but hell, I just couldn't see to load otherwise. The first evening I was there, I was assigned a cot in a hootch with some 2/1 grunts. They were good people. 2/1 had a chow hall and NCOs had head of line privileges. L/Cpl's and below carried rifles to chow, NCOs wore pistols. The grunt squad leader would lend me his pistol belt and I would go to the front of the line and get in and out faster, freeing me up to get back loading quicker. I didn't go to the chow hall every day; a lot of times I would shut down and have some C's or long rats. 2/1 was also changing areas during the time I was there, with who, I can't remember. One of the other regiments were flip-flopping areas with them, and some of my Shore Party friends would be in the area now and again, unloading and loading gear. I was assigned to Amtracs only, but if we had time we would help each other. 2/1 had a strange area. On one hand, it seemed real safe; on the other it had more snipers harassing it than almost any other area I'd been to. One side of the perimeter had some old blown up, burnt-out, Amtracs a few hundred yards, give or take from it, and Charlie liked to slip inside those old hulls and take pot shots at the area. The Motor Transport Shop was next to the perimeter and they had an

M-60 real handy, so when a sniper got too aggravating, they would stop working, grab it, and hose the old hulls down. That would secure the sniping for a while. I stepped out of the hootch one afternoon, about 1 p.m. and damn near got a haircut. The Motor-T boys brought out their sixty and secured that shit. But probably the strangest thing about their area was, across from their compound, carved right into the side of the mountain, was a Buddhist pagoda, steps carved out of stone ran right up to it. The 2/1 Marines had guns zeroed in on it and Charlie knew it, but regardless, Old Victor Charles and his Northern cousins, the N.V.A., would attempt, from time to time, to sneak up those stairs to do whatever it is they do up there. When they tried it, the sound of a single round from a 50 ca. could be heard, a tracer round used as a marking round, followed by the loud boom of a 106 recoilless rifle. Sometimes that would repeat over again a few times and in the morning the rumors would fly about how many kills they got on the mountain last night. Near the end of my stay there, I was working after dark in the lot where all of Amtrac's gear that was left was staged. A fellow operator and friend, from Shore Party who was working for 2/1, came over to shoot the bull. I shut down and he hopped up on the lift. We were facing the wire, but you couldn't see anything, it was a pitch-black night. What happened next was our own damn fault, we knew better, but we were both dead tired from loading and unloading. We were sitting up on the lift relaxing and telling each other lies and jokes and we were both smoking. Now, my dear friend, the lit end of a cigarette glowing in the dark can be seen from distances you wouldn't believe. An RTF 6000 Pettibone only has one seat, which I was occupying, and Pauly, my buddy, was sitting on the sheet metal between the controls and the fuel tank, probably two feet tops between us. The round parted the air between us, not over our heads, but right between us. I felt a blast of air against my cheek. I looked over at Pauly, he looked at me, neither one of us spoke or made any gestures, but at the same time he leaned right and I leaned left, letting my weight take me right off onto the ground. There was a thud sound as our bodies smacked the ground hard. Neither one of us tried to block our fall. I landed hard on my left side, he on his right. I crouched up and made my way along the side to the back of the lift. Pauly did the same. So, there we were hiding behind the machine. I said, "Hey, Pauly, go get our rifles, okay?" (they were still up on the lift). He laughed and suggested I get them. It was a sniper and not an attack, so we just kicked back behind the lift for a while. The sniper wasn't accurate anymore; a few more rounds snapped overhead, but nothing too close anymore. One of the Amtrac LT.'s was in front of his warehouse and yelled over asking if we were alright. We yelled back that we were cool. About half hour later I went to loading flatbeds. I had to get them ready to be pulled out bright and early. I finished up about two days later and on schedule and when the LT. released me he handed me an envelope addressed to the Commanding Officer, 1st Shore Party Bn. Inside was a letter making me sound like the most squared away, hardest working forklift jock in Eye Corps, and what a fine representative of 1st S.P. Bn. I was, and that I should be commended in whatever way my C.O. saw fit. First letter of any kind I had ever received and I was a foot taller when I left their area. I know it's corny, but I was real proud of it. When I got back to Shore Party's Rear, it was about quarter to six. The chow hall closed at six, so I parked the lift on the heavy equipment lot and ran for the chow hall. I ran head on into S/Sgt. Millen, my platoon Sgt. I gave him my letter and asked him if he would get it to the C.O. He assured me he would, and I burst through the chow hall door in time to get a hot meal. The next day down at the heavy junk lot, I asked S/Sgt. Millen (I, by the way, was an 18 year old L/Cpl. with just a little over one year in the Corps.) if he had taken care of my letter. He said, "Yeah, Top's got it." I didn't hear any more about it. About a week later I asked our dispatcher, who had his desk outside Top's office, if he had any scoop on the letter I got from Amtrac's. He said "Yeah, Top's got it." I asked a couple more times over the next month and I always go the same reply, "Top's got it." "Top's taking care of it." I was too much of a boot to know about requesting Mast and was nervous as hell even talking to anyone with brass or heavy chevrons so, "Top's got it," period. Hurt my motivation and morale, I'll tell you that, it hurt man. I know its bullshit, "don't mean nothing." Why hell, 50¢ and that letter, I could get a cup of coffee. But, between you and me, it hurt bro, it hurt. I guess Top's still got it. I hope he got whatever he wanted to get out of it. Semper Fi right, yeah right, Top.

THE BRIDGE

OKAY, WELL, LET'S talk about the bridge, don't want to, you understand, but maybe you'll need to hear it and I know deep down I need to write it. On the backside of Hill 55 was a bridge across the river, I don't know. If the bridge had a name, I can't remember that either. Bridge security was pretty tight. Charlie loved blow bridges. The troops on the bridge would drop concussion grenades in the water every 20 minutes or so to take care of any swimming bad guys and anything that floated down that river was fired upon. On the friendly side of the bridge, you could wash clothes and equipment and bathe your bod. So yours truly used to don a pair of tiger shorts and grab my M-16 and a couple bandoliers of ammo and take my lift down to the bridge, most days around 4 p.m. I liked to bathe on one side and fire into the river on the other. The guards on the bridge didn't mind the help shooting at floating stuff. There was village, on the right bank, not too far upstream. I noticed nobody paid any attention to what people were shooting at, so, yeah, you guessed it, Marines started popping a round off into the village now and again. Of course it seemed to me to make perfect sense back then, but after I got sober, it started working on my mind some, it may have always bothered me, but the self-medication of drugs and alcohol numbed it. I told myself those villages were helping the V.C. anyway. When I left 55 for a couple of weeks back at Shore Party's rear, I got stuck on a month's perimeter guard duty and yes, race fans, Marines I know started firing at Vietnamese folks. A little different way this time. There was a day and night post near the edge of a well-traveled road (part of Route 1, I believe). Well, they would load one round at a time and when a loud vehicle passed, they would snipe at Papa-sans working their paddies. The passing vehicle drowned out the sound of the shot. Daytime only, no traffic at night, no one in the paddie, least no one who shouldn't be shot at. I don't believe this story is going anywhere, I just had to put it down. So, later folks. I've got a pounding, painful, throbbing in my right temple. I'm sorry 'bout that. The shooting that is, not my temple.

SHORE PARTY
FREEDOM HILL

B ACK IN THE rear, it really sucks. They want us to start saluting. Well if they want to be known as officers it's alright with me. Can't stand the rear, so what do I do. Volunteer for perimeter guard duty of course. It's better than going on forklift runs to the Navy Seabees lumber yard or division PX. At least I get to play Marine even if it is the rear. We have guard school every day at 1600. Where we're informed on the intelligent reports about every activity in our area. So we know whether to have 50% up or 100% awake. Some of those reports were wild, an all-woman sapper plt. on the move 100% alert. Okay, if they say so. I was on a reactionary platoon. (which is part of guard). We used to take the Corpsman out to the village a couple of clicks away. We walked in a patrol formation to the village then made a 360° around it, while the Corpsman went in and treated the people. Well, this village had a

38

rough puff platoon. Rough Puffs were Vietnamese militia. They wanted to be inspected by our dai-uy (captain) so yours truly was picked and the captain and I went into their compound. They were in formation. What a group Marine corps cammies, tiger strip cammies, half black PJ's, half cammie uniform. A real rag-tag bunch, and their weapons, grease guns, M-14's, M-1 carbines, AK47's and one or two M-16's. Well, we inspected them and the captain told their officer how sharp they were. I'll be damned if they didn't give the Capt. and I cold Cokes in bottles. Man, what a treat on a hot autumn. We walked on patrol back to our base without incident, except for one angry water buffalo who got a little close to us. Everyone was on full auto, at least I was until it passed a little Viet boy on its back. Us POG's felt like real Marines for a little while. Thank goodness nothing happened. Another good day in Nam. On the perimeter the next day we were drunk or had been drinking and some guy had been smoking some. It was common in the rear. We did not get high or drunk on forward fire bases. But it happened in Freedom Hill rear. Well, we had four conditions. Condition one, under attack, condition two, waiting for attack, condition three, fairly safe and condition four, normal. These conditions changed daily and the guard personnel had to know them. The O.D. (officer of day) would check posts throughout the night. The smart ones did not try and sneak up on you. Well, one night we were high, the radio was blasting the Rolling Stones, 'Gimme Shelter' and we were talking loud and laughing in the small 15 foot tower we were in. The O.D. came up the ladder without us hearing or feeling it. He came in and said, "What condition are you Marines in?" Of course he meant condition one and four. We looked at each other and a Marine we called 'Hot Rod' said, "We're fucked up, Sir." Oh hell, we're all busted now. The O.D. said keep the radio down to a roar and you are in condition four. It was only 1830. He left and we felt like throwing Hot Rod out of the tower, but didn't. Another day marked off my calendar.

GOING HOME

I SAW IT TIME after time, a Marine was eligible for R&R after six months in country. Guys would go after seven months or so and come back and be real depressed 'cause they couldn't leave again for five months. I was not going to let this happen to me. I figured I'd go on R&R in my 10th or 11th month. Then when I came back I would be happy 'cause I would be a short-timer. So like I've said here before, I hated the rear. Let me clarify, I liked landing zones and FSB's. They were rear areas to the grunts, and forward bases to us POG's. So I was at Freedom Hill filling sandbags and word came they needed three men (two for LZ Baldy, Hill 63) and one for FSB Ross (Hill 51, 10 miles SW of Baldy). Baldy didn't seem that bad to me but I really did not want to go to Ross. Ross was in a really bad neighborhood. The Que-sohn Valley, avery bad place. But better than the chicken shit back at Freedom Hill, right? I volunteered to go and was accepted. I went with two buddies who were senior in Nam to me. They had both been on operations on Go-Noi Island, Dodge City

area. I had not. So I got picked for Ross and they got picked for LZ Baldy.

We flew out to LZ Baldy by chopper from Da-Nang's 1st Recon LZ. We

were excited and glad we were getting away from garrison-type duties.

Baldy was great. We had a nice little equipment lot and a big hootch.

You worked at important stuff all day, supplying the grunts not PM'ing

gear and doing mess duty and boring things. Well, we did PM but when

needed; not as busy work like in Freedom Hill. Well, after three days,

guess what, it was time for me to chopper over to FSB Ross (30 miles

South of Da-Nang). Okay I was scared, but tried to act together. This

was TET of 1970. TET of 1968 had been bad. No one knew from year

to year what TET might bring. Bad time, bad neighborhood. Bad nerves!

We lived in a tent, slept with our clothes and boots on and a round in

the chamber. Had never been on a fire base where I slept with a round in

the chamber. That was SOP at Ross. I was responsible for unloading and

loading supplies on the LZ. My lift a piece of crap. It had no brakes and

would not lift the 6,000 lbs. it was supposed to. I tried to dead line it one

time until I could get the brakes fixed. Well, the grunts were unloading a

truck of ammo by hand, which I hadn't even noticed, and a captain bust in the tent and said, "Where's the lift operator?" I said, "Here." He said, "Go unload that truck." I told him the lift was down cause of brakes. He said, "What's the matter, you got no balls?!" Well, needless to say, I went right out and unloaded the ammo and never tried to dead line the gear again. I was told you never run gear that's broke; it'll just get worse, but not at Ross. We definitely improvised. We did everything with nothing or broken stuff. Everything here was important and to be done now. By the way, an old Top came by the hootch and told me his captain didn't know how to talk to troops and gave me a case of warm soda. Which we drank and washed my butt-hurt away. We had two Army guys in the tent with us. They were Americal DIV grunts, one had a confirmed kill when Ross was overrun. They ran our water point, which is they unloaded our water jugs brought in each day by an Army Chinook chopper. Everything just about came to Ross by air. The roads in and out were real bad. We tried to get a better lift form Shore Party rear, by lowboy but the truck never made it. Well, I was out on the LZ working. I had 10 months in country now. I was getting short. The radio operator came up to me and asked my service number. I gave it to him and he said, "You get on the next chopper back to Da-Nang, you're going home." How could that be?

He said, "You gonna argue?" I said, "Hell, no." Twenty minutes later I

was packed and at the LZ waiting the Da-Nang bird. Back in Da-Nang

you found out about Nixon's pullout of units by seniority. 1st Shore Party,

1st Marine Division was next on the list. About three weeks later, I was

onboard the USS Tulare, aka cargo ship, headed non-stop to San Diego.

A month of the Pacific Ocean and I was at Camp Pendleton being offered

a six month early out from the Corps. What a ride folks, what a ride!!!

PART II

PART II

COMING HOME

AT LAST, I got to pinch myself. April 10, 1970. It's like 3 p.m. and I'm in L.A.X. looking at all these beautiful long-legged women. About 10 a.m. this morning, a Marine Major shook my hand and said, "Thanks for your service, see 'ya in the next one." Then he handed me a package containing my separation papers from Uncle Sam's misguided children. Back then if you wanted to fly military stand-by and get a discount on your fare, you had to fly in uniform, so I was all decked out in my dress greens, razor sharp creases, new emblems and new ribbons I'd never worn before. I'm a vet now and I do admit standing around the airport, I felt kinda salty, even put a little dip in the middle of my piss cutter. There's the call for my flight, flip the old sea bag up on my right shoulder and off I go. Damn thing weights a ton, but I'll be damned if I let on like it does. Pride, baby, pride; check bag at counter and board that beautiful bird. Don't crash now baby, please, this is my last flight. Man, everything is better somehow, colors are brighter, smells sweeter, sounds clearer and round-eyed American women are more gorgeous than I ever remember. In about three hours or so, I'll be walking through O'Hara Airport and then a 30 minute cab ride and I'll be home; seems so unreal, HOME, yeah! Wheels up, climbing, all those scary noises and shuttering-type movements, these babies make and they're all leveled out, beautiful blue sky, sink back in the seat, relax and I'm ready for a drink and then maybe a nap, if I can, I'm so excited! Here she comes, she's an angel dressed in dark blue stew's uniform, glad I got an aisle seat. What should I have? Vodka, bourbon or Manhattan? Yeah, a Manhattan. I believe that's what I had on the flight to California's a year ago. The good-looking stew leans over in from of me and says, "Coffee, milk or soft drink?" "No, I'd like a Manhat—." She cuts me off in mid-sentence says rather hatefully, "You weren't listening; coffee, milk or soft drink?" I swear she had a look of pure hate in those pretty eyes. "Oh, um, nothing then, thank you," I embarrassingly said. She turned away quickly without saying a word. I know I'm not 21 yet, but airlines always served me in uniform before, and, damn that look she gave me, and the mean sound of her voice really floored me. I sat quietly the rest of the flight and didn't look at or talk to anyone. Walking through O'Hare, I thought I caught a few hateful looks from folks, but maybe that stew had just made me paranoid. Out into the refreshing night air, I felt good, hopped in the first cab and off we went. I was like a little kid with my face to the back window, trying to see everything we passed. Then he started, "Just coming home?" "Yeah," I say. "Viet-nam?" he said. "Yeah," I said. "Let me tell you about Viet-nam," he said. And he did, the entire damn trip, he went on and on about the moral and political wrongs of Viet-nam conflict, as he called it. I don't tell him to shut up, I don't argue with him, I just sat back there hoping the ride would end, I mean, I don't care right now. I'm home, I want to celebrate. Instead, all I'm getting is hateful stares, rude stews and this cabbie's fucking moral and political views; and the insinuation that I'm a big fool for going. I got to get out of this uniform. I throw the money at the driver, run up the stairs of our house, shedding my greens as I go. My brother opens the door and I race to the bedroom and change into civvie's. My mother says, "Oh son, I wanted to see you in uniform!" I mumble something about putting it on again later. It was a strange homecoming. They seemed uneasy and didn't know quite what

49

to say to me. I felt that way too, plus I couldn't help wondering if they weren't looking at me like maybe I was a little bit nuts. As the days and months passed by and I still wouldn't call friends or go outside; I realize now, Mom did believe her son had maybe lost a marble or two. I had to get ready for this new world, that's all; I just needed a little time to adjust. You know, it's funny, as I sit here years later, I'm wondering just how long it's gonna take!

FIRST TIME OUT

WASN'T REALLY MY first time out. I'd been sneaking out
in the wee hours for a couple of weeks, but it was my first
official going out. I wasn't ready yet, but a couple friends I'd grown up
with had finally found out, somehow, that I was back and staying in.
Probably my mother told them, she must have been worried, after all,
I had been holed up at home three or four months now. So, over they
come, with plenty of questions. "How come you didn't let us know you
were back, etc.?" "Get some shoes on and let's go out." "No, no," I say,
"Let's just sit here and visit." "Bullshit buddy, get some damn shoes on
and let's go!" I didn't have any shoes. I had my black Marine Corps shoes
and boots, so I put on my beat-up jungle boots. "Damn, ain't you got
nothing but those, they look like they been through a fucking war!"
"Nope, that's all I got," I said. I dunno, I didn't think they looked that
bad. "Well, okay then," they say, "Screw it, let's go." So out we go and

pile in their car. They're laughing and feel at ease and don't seem to have a care in the world. Well, I'll tell you something. I was nervous as hell and felt like a visitor from another planet. I should explain a little something here. When I left home, everybody was what you would call 'greasers,' I guess. Bunch of phony tough guys drinking booze and smoking cigarettes. Now they had long hair and bell bottom jeans and were drinking wine and smoking pot. Their way of talking, music and hell, just about everything was different. So we went to a friend's home where there was always a party of some type going on. There I ran into two more friends and I find out one is AWOL from the Army and the other is in Deserter status from the Navy. The two buddies I left the house with had been lucky with the draft lottery. So we kick back and smoke some weed and drink some wine. They start bringing me up to date on what they've been doing since I left, which seemed to me to be nothing but a bunch of childish nonsense. I was also having trouble inside with the fact that two old buddies were now cowardly deserters, in my book. I tried not to show it, of course, then in comes Ben. Ben is the Casanova of the neighborhood and always has a different girlfriend, all of them pretty and dumb. So it goes, "Hey man, welcome back." "Hi

Ben, good to see 'ya, man." To his girl he says, "This is my buddy. He just got back from Nam." His girl says, "Yeah well, that's his fucking problem, ain't it?" "Hey," Ben yells, "Shut the fuck up, this my friend. "Sorry," he says to me. She butts in and says, "How many women and kids did you kill?" Ben starts yelling at her again and I say, "Hey Ben, it's okay man, don't worry about it. Good to see 'ya." I went out to get some air. My friend Robbie comes out and says, "Hey man, come on back in, she promises she won't say nothing no more." "Nah, maybe you could drive me home." And he did. I got back in the house and felt safe again. I knew I wasn't ready to go out yet but I had almost forgotten why. Oh, I remember now though, oh yes. I remember real good now. It's the ambushes. Everything looks okay until you walk into it and then they really let you have it. You know, it's funny she asked me how many women and kids I had killed. She should have known that women were capable of attacking and killing American troops, after all, she had just opened fire on me. But, I didn't kill her. I knew the difference between peace and war back then. I guess she didn't. Oh well, let me go to my room and get something for this pain.

THOUGHTS YOU
SHOULDN'T HAVE

Have you ever?

I have.

Sometimes.

I used to make secret forays.

Into the early morning hours

When the streets were quiet.

No people

I'd think

I'll give 'em nuts.

I'll hurt 'em.

I'll hurt every fucking one of them.

I'll get these ignorant soft mothers.

I'll become a long hair.

HA.

Fuck with this long hair.

I won't give you a flower,

I'll give you a fucking knuckle sandwich or worse.

I might just shoot your ass.

IN COMING

Oh shit. Get, man, get.

Same life draining, heart pounding fear

Hurry, hurry get moving

Finally my feet make contact and I'm booking.

Running, oh yes, much better, this running

I thought I was too slow getting up, thought I was too late.

Whoom, Flash, Stop, Quick!

Don't run into it!

Ouch! OOOHH!

Shit what was that?

A table?

Outside?

Daze, fog, confusion

Awake now, toe hurts, sweating

Things starting to take shape

Feel cold

Feel really frigging strange.

I wanna get back to bed before they see me.

Hope it doesn't storm all night.

CHICAGO 1970

S HE WAS BEAUTIFUL. I was young and strong and hip. She was next to me at the bar. The 'My Way,' I believe it was called. My friend and I had spotted her and her friend in traffic. We had followed them in the lounge. Did I say she was beautiful? She looked like an angel. She actually sat down next to me. We talked and talked. I was on top of the world. We were hitting it off wonderfully.

DA-NANG 1969

Papa-san says, "Number one job, hey #1. What you think, number one job, right?" "Yes, Papa-san, #1 job." And it was. He had just engraved my Zippo lighter. My name on top and USMC, Viet-Nam, '69-'70 on the bottom. I loved that lighter.

CHICAGO 1970

She picked up my lighter and lit one of those long, female-type smokes. She gave me a funny look and sat it back down. "Were you in Viet-nam?" "Yeah," was all I said. "That's a shame," she said, "I could never like you." "What?" I said. "You heard me, you're a murderer, get lost!" and she stormed away. I told my buddie Al, "Let's go." "Why?" he said. "Just let's go," and out I went, in a hurry. We drove around for a while when I realized my Zippo was still in the bar, so back we went. The place was closed. I banged on the door until the bartender opened up and I got my lighter and left. I had grown long hair trying to fit in. There was a bar that catered to an older crowd next door and two fellows, I'd say in their early to mid-40's, were standing around holding up parking meters. When I walked past, one said to his buddy, "Look at this shit." I snapped. I hit him with a right with all the anger and force I could muster. He fell into the street and I dived on top, punching and punching. Al had to pull me off and we booked. I believe I was really starting to strongly dislike civilians.

PEOPLE

People-clean, fresh, busy, laughing, playing,

Threatening, starting, accusing

They're different. I don't remember this.

I stay inside, the sidewalk hurts my feet.

Sometimes I go out at night.

I drive all night.

I'm barefoot.

I don't have a license.

My brother's car, he doesn't know, or he does,

And pretends he doesn't.

I drink a lot these days.

Somebody might be watching this house.

I'll face the people.

I'll join them,

Somehow.

I can be like them.

I'll learn.

I'll change.

Not today, maybe tomorrow,

I will belong again.

PARTY TIME

MY GIRLFRIEND'S BOSS called me up, 'cause I wanted my girl to come over instead of attending their stupid office party. "Hello, how are you? I heard you are recently back from Nam, huh?" "Yeah." "Were you up on the front line?" "Well, it was kinda confusing as far as a front." "Well hey, look, why don't you come on down. We got plenty of food and drink. Join on in." I say, "Sorry, I can't make it man. Thanks anyway, though." To myself I'm thinking, "This ignorant S.O.B. The war has been going on for five years and people don't know jack about it. Nobody cares man, nobody fucking cares." I felt like going down there and killing every suit in the place. Oh well, time for meds. Roll that joint, bro. Roll that joint and don't think about it. Peace man, peace.

GAINFUL EMPLOYMENT

Forest Park, IL. 1973

I HAD LANDED MYSELF a pretty good job at a Hydraulic Jack Co. I ran a forklift most of the time and an overhead crane the rest. I enjoyed that and the pay was pretty good. The hours were 7 a.m. till 3 p.m. I liked getting off by 3 p.m. I never wore uniform trousers or shirt to work, but jungle boots were comfortable work shoes. We didn't have a lunchroom; we just ate wherever we were when lunch break came. On my third day there, I was sitting on a pallet eating, when about six of the fellows who worked there (all about my age) came over. They all stood around me and the spokesman for the group said, "Hey man, me and the guys would like to ask you a question." "Yeah, sure, what is it?" "Well, we were wondering where you got them boots." "Oh," I replied, "in the service." "Which service?" "I was with the Marines." "Oh yeah, how come you don't talk about it like Danny does?" I don't know is all I said. I had seen Danny a couple of times when I was standing around waiting to clock out. Danny was a loud mouth braggart and from the few stories I heard him telling, he was also full of shit. "Yeah," so the spokesman says, "Them are jungle boots like they use in Viet-nam aren't they?" I say, "Yeah." He says what I knew he would. "Were you in Viet-nam?" Well, folks, here goes, maybe they'll say "Welcome home man." Yeah, he, that would be great. So he says, "Well, me and the guys here just want you to know that we would have gone to Viet-nam too, but we don't dig killing people, you got that?" Yeah man, I got it. I got it all right; I got it again, straight through the heart like a hot knife. Course I didn't say that, I said, "Yeah, okay." And they walked away while I sat there bleeding from another welcome back wound. Thinking, "Yeah, you don't like killing people, what you assholes really mean is that you're misinformed, unpatriotic, chicken mother f'ers." I also had a fleeting thought that they were walking away all nice and bunched up together and that one frag would wax them all. Course, I didn't have a frag handy so I continued to work there two weeks in complete silence. No one spoke to me and I spoke to no one. That got to me, so out the door I went. The boss thought I was a complete deadbeat, I'm sure. Guess I'll have to remember not to wear jungle boots to my next job. They're just not as comfortable as they used to be.

ANOTHER DAY

Fantasize, wish, hope, worry, despair, anticipate?

Anticipate.

Yeah, anticipate. Anticipate what?

New love, gloom, disaster, death?

Yesterday's gone!

Tomorrow's too late!

Today, another day, will it happen today?

What? I don't know, but it won't be good, that's a given.

I'll survive.

That's the problem. I always survive.

But a piece is always taken.

Whittled down until there's nothing left.

THE HALL

YOU EVER GO in a V.F.W. post? I did once. I was dating a girl whose Daddy was Post Commander. She had to stop in and pick up some keys. "Come in with me." "Naw," I said, "I'll wait here in the car." Daddy didn't approve of me. "Come on, please?" she purred. "Oh, okay." So we sat at the bar and her Dad sets us up with a couple of beers and gives her the keys (I still had long hair). So her old man is talking to her, ignoring me as usual and some old guy walks past behind us and says to her Dad, "Well, I see your two daughters are visiting tonight." That one everybody enjoyed and everyone laughed except my date, thank goodness. I didn't say a word, I just sipped my beer and stared straight ahead wondering if any of those yo-yo's would be stupid enough to touch me. After the laughter had died down, her Daddy says, "Now John, that's not nice, this here is my daughter's friend and he's one of them Viet-nam vets." "Oh, yeah," John said, "I've heard of them, messed everything up and lost, didn't they?" A lot of yeah's and Amen's went around the room. I took my date's arm and off we went, her apologizing for the way they acted. I never did go into another V.F.W. after that. I don't believe I'll ever become a member. You know, it's funny. When I was in Nam I used to think, "If I make it home, I'll be able to join the V.F.W." Oh well, don't mean nothing.

HOME SWEET HOME

SIT WHERE I can see exits and nobody can come up behind me.
For a long time I did this without realizing it. Now I do. Funny I
still do it.

I walk along and sometimes I watch out for mines. Why?

I look for possible ambush sites as I drive along.

Do you ever wonder what happened to some of the people, the children?

Do you own a Starlite Scope?

I can't afford one.

Does the sunlight hurt your eyes?

I don't like wearing shades.

Do your clothes feel and fit funny?

Eric Koplin

Do people stare at you?

Are they really?

I watch for danger signs. I don't like crowds.

Was somebody talking to you and you weren't there?

Did you hear choppers today?

Where are your jungle boots?

Are you bitter? Angry?

Does everything look unreal?

Phony even?

Do you still want to go home?

DREAMS 1995

'M IN WASHINGTON, D.C. I'm across the street from the Viet-nam museum. It's a very large government building. It has an N.V.A. flag flying out front. There are tourists from all over the world lined up to get in. I'm across the street watching the lines moving in and people coming out with pamphlets and brochures. I'm crying, not bawling, but my eyes are wet and my heart aches. I cross the street and get in line. The line is mostly young people, high school and college students. I get inside and it's a history museum full of Commie propaganda, books and file cabinets, pictures on the walls all glorifying the N.V.A. and V.C. forces. Pictures of Communist forces helping the people and pictures of U.S. forces committing all sorts of atrocities against the peace-loving people of Viet-nam. The U.S. students and tourists are eating it all up. I'm crying good now and trying to tell people this is not true. I'm forced out of the building by security guards. I'm walking down the block crying and people are passing by talking about how nice the N.V.A. were and how U.S. forces really hurt that poor country. I get to the corner and I'm confronted by a gang of touch street kids. I run, the street kids chasing me. I finally lose them and turn a corner and there's a group of Vets around a garbage can fire. "Hey bro," they yell, "Over here." So I go over there and feel safe and secure. They say, "Join us bro. We know what to do." They start blowing their brains out one by one. I'm screaming, "No, no, don't!" They just keep shooting themselves. I wake up. I feel like I've been crying in my sleep.

MY AREA

'M RESPONSIBLE. I'M wary, a little scared. I know I'm home. I think? I must keep watch. They're so irresponsible, these people. They don't need guarded, they think. I must keep watch. They sleep so well. I check my weapon, can't be too careful. I know my area, I know the terrain. Every woodpile, every garbage can. Penny the lab helps, she watches too. Why does she watch? Does she know I do? I'm tired, I can't hear as well anymore. My eyes, well, I know some tricks. I scan, the area, back and forth. Don't stare at nothing. Which way will they come? Damn single shot. I hate it. Never the right gear. No flares, no wire, no fighting holes. Too much area for one man. I'm fucked, I think. I wonder why I do it. No one cares, they don't know. Must have dozed off around three. Noises don't wake me like they used to. Hope they don't come between five and six. Worry about the time. Got to go to work soon. Full moon tomorrow. Maybe I can sleep. Hey, maybe it'll end. Maybe it'll be over, yeah right, and maybe. Just maybe. Maybe. Just maybe.

DREAMS

COMMON DREAM I have a lot. Someone is breaking into the house. I hear them and I have a weapon within reach but I'm frozen. I can't speak, I can't move. I hear them coming, getting closer and closer. I can't move. I'm straining with all my might, but I can't move. Then I wake up. When I'm awake, I'm terrified to find out I'm the same way. I really am paralyzed and I lay there fighting it, wondering if someone really is in the house. Finally, after what seems an eternity, I break free, but I can't move fast. I'm groggy and feel like I'm moving underwater. I roam the house with a shotgun until I'm convinced it was the dream again. Sometimes I can't go back to sleep and I stand guard until daylight. Better safe than sorry or is that paranoia?

CONVERSATIONS
AND THOUGHTS

MY WIFE SAYS, "I can hardly see in here, it's so dark." "What?" I reply. She says, "Dark like Viet-nam." I get chills and a panic feeling. I say, "What!" She says, "It's dark without the lamp." She swears she never said a thing about Viet-nam. I'm driving the work truck with my partner Gary. I turn in towards the main P.X. and as I round the corner I say, "Going to visit a buddy." He says, "What?" I thought he asked where I was going. He swears he never said a word. Then I realize, I don't know anybody here. So, why am I here and why did I say such a thing? Admiral Armadillo Poo Poo, the name just came to me. I find myself wondering how the Admiral would handle certain situations and I'll use his solutions. At the same time, I feel this is crazy, but thoughts of this Admiral keep popping up. Is it my meds? Am I losing my mind? My shrink says, "Don't worry about it, it's just stress."

DREAM

'M STANDING ON a road in Viet-nam near a post I used to man from time to time. Out of the middle of the road comes a large beam and inside is a Marine in combat gear. He's waving to me to come inside the beam. I try, but it's like a force field, I can't reach through it. He goes floating up the beam and disappears. Another Marine comes up out of the ground into the beam. He tries to get out, but can't and then floats up. They start coming faster now. One at a time they float up and away. Some are real pissed at me and try kicking and punching me through the beam. I can't hear their voices, but I can tell they're cursing at me. Some are friendly wanting me to enter the beam, some want to kick my ass. Scene changes and I'm walking down the road and I approach a Marine squad set up in a defensive position on the roadside. I yell, "Hey guys!" and they look at me and open fire. I wake up startled and sweating and afraid.

ESCAPE

YOU KNOW, ONE of the things we love so much about being Americans is that you can travel. You got the money and you want to go, then go ahead man, make your hat. I've been thinking a lot lately about doing just that. Just leave it all behind; just hit the road that's sung about so much. Like Paul Simon said, "Just get on the bus, Gus." Now, one mode of travel that is romantic and adventurous and truly American is the Harley Davidson. Yes sir, I've been thinking about getting a motorcycle and just hitting the road to the unknown. Wind in my hair, the skin on my face stretched back from the blast of. I don't have any money right now so I can't buy a new Harley, so I'm thinking about other motorcycles. I've come to the conclusion that a lot of things can be your motorcycle out of here to the unknown. Maybe if I got my little four cylinder car going fast enough and knocked out the windshield, then I would feel the wind in my hair and my skin would stretch back from the blast and I'd be on the road outta here. Or maybe a 12-guage motorcycle? You could even kick start it with your foot and your hair would stand up and your face would stretch back from the blast and you would be on the road going to some new, adventurous, unknown destination. Yes sir, motorcycles are the way out. I could escape on a motorcycle. Man, this country is great, freedom to travel, just hop on your motorcycle and go, bro, go! I'll find the right motorcycle one of these days. It can't be any old one, it's gotta be one I'll get a real blast out of. Did you ever ride a motorcycle? Think you ever will? Well, later. I got to look around for a fast one.

IMPENDING DOOM

EVER HAVE IT? I have. Once, a long time ago it came over me and like a misty fog, it hung there for days. And like the fog, it slipped away, not to stay gone. No, I couldn't be that lucky. It comes back to visit, to let me know it knows me. Lately it visits me a lot. Do you get used to yours? I don't, I tried making it my friend, an omen I could count on. But no, my foggy doom can't be trusted. Won't be a friend. I have to ditch it, find somewhere in my mind I can go, where it won't follow. I wish it would stand and fight. Like a knight, I would slay it, hold it up, and damn it. But my doom won't fight, just visit from time to time to make sure I'm not enjoying myself too much. Nasty thing that it is. Do you ever feel it, my friend? I hope and pray not. Wish me luck, I'll outsmart it yet.

MY DEMON

THE DEMON FOOLED me again. His buddy, Impending Doom came first. I fought with him. Victory was mine. I had hope, I had a goal. I let my defenses down. I didn't feel the demon. I didn't know he was inside me again. Was he there all the time waiting? Did he leave only to return when the time was right? I was so close this time, so close. I fell out, couldn't move, couldn't shave, or bathe, or eat or care at all. I couldn't stop him. He slipped my body on. It fits him like a well-tailored suit. His 'rage outfit.' Dressed as me, out he goes. Let's rock and roll, my man. A little abuse. A little damage. Some torture, terror, evil and tonight, just maybe tonight, a DEATH! I felt the weight of the weapon in my hand and realized I had it. I sat down and told him "Get out, get the fuck out!" He left laughing. I'm still drained. I don't care anymore. If I have hope or goals or dreams, he'll be back. I don't know if I can stop him again. I'm tired. Tired of rage. Tired of violence. Tired of the fight. I'm giving a lot of thought to surrendering, but! I mean, just maybe. Yeah, just maybe, one more go at it. What'll you say, bro? Let's give one more go!

TOWER CLIMBER

MAN, I'M SORRY, but I understand that. I've felt that way myself. Just fuck people up, fuck 'em. They treated us like shit. Just blow their asses away. I don't care for the outcome of it, though. Hurting innocent people sucks, they have people who love them. Killing anything you don't have to is bad news! Plus, you're going out or to jail. That's not cool. Maybe just a high-powered BB gun. I've thought of that, but hell, those things hurt people too. I told the people at work I was gonna blow them away. I meant it too. Then a little later I realized I really didn't want to and was sorry I said it. Hell, I was scared I said it, 'cause I was losing control. I saw some professional people about it and they said I was stressed out, that I was probably stressed out for years. PTSD, they call it. I felt better that you could put a name to it, 'cause I just felt crazy, crazy frigging Vet. They type the newspapers love to write about. Well, I'm getting help now. Least I believe its help, we'll see. I'll let you know if it does. Later people got to take my meds.

UNDER DOCTOR'S CARE

February Years Later

D O YOU LIKE being greeted? With big smiling faces? In the hospital they greet you every morning. They say, "Good morning," in their sing-song voices, "How are you feeling?" I start to tell them and they cut me off. "We'll see to you today. Oh yes, we'll see to your every need." They write on charts that nobody can see and nobody reads.

GLOSSARY

#1 & #10	pidgin, #1 being the best, #10 being the worst
106	recoilless rifle
2/1	2nd Battalion, 1st Marine Regiment
471	SuperCharger
50 cal.	heavy duty machine gun
7-82 gear	combat gear, includes ammo pouches, first aid kit & etc.
AK-47	Communist standard rifle
Amtrac	amphibious tractor
Baby-san	pidgin for any unmarried Vietnamese
Beetlenut	A mild narcotic plant the Vietnamese chew which leaves their teeth and gums stained red
Bird	any airplane or helicopter
Book	to leave in a hurry
Cammies	camouflage uniforms
Charlie	VC
Choppers	helicopters

C-Rats	U.S. rations
Dead Line	put out of service
Dog Patch	a village known for its drugs and prostitutes
F4 Phantom	U.S. fighter aircraft
FNG	fucking new guy
Frags	fragmentation grenade
FSB's	fire support bases
Gooks	Vietnamese people
Gook Sores	jungle rot
Grunts	infantry
Headache Bar	rollover protection; roll bar
Heavy Junk	slang term for Military Heavy Equipment
Ho Chi Mein Sandals	sandals made from old tires
Hootch	any dwelling; in most cases a wooden hut
HST	helo support teams
I Corps	Northern-most military zone, pronounced "eye" corps
L/Cpl.	Lance Corporal E3
Long Rats	long range patrol rations; dehydrated meals
L.T.	Lieutenant
M-16	U.S. standard rifle
M-60	a machine gun
Make your hat	to leave; to boogie
Mama-san	pidgin for all married Vietnamese women
M.P.C.	Military Payment Certificate

NCO	Non-Commissioned Officer
NVA	North Vietnamese regular Army
O.D.	officer of day
Oki	Okinawa
One Click	about a thousand meters
Papa-san	pidgin for any married Vietnamese male
Piss Cutter	Marine Corps Service cap
POG	support type troop
Pop-Up	a hand-held flare
POV	personal operated vehicle
P.X.	Post Exchange
RPG	Rocket Propelled Grenade
RTF 6000	Rough Terrain Forklift
Salty	a seasoned Marine
Sgt.	Sergeant E5
S/Sgt.	Staff Sergeant E6
Shitbird	poor excuse for a Marine
Short timer	Marine with 90 days or less
Top	Master Sergeant E8
VC	the enemy
XO	Executive Officer

Fire Support Base Ross 1970

Fire Support Base Ross 1970

Landing Zone Baldy 1970

Hill 55 1969

Freedom Hill 1969

Your author 1969